CELEBRATING THE CITY OF MAKKAH

Celebrating the City of Makkah

Walter the Educator

Silent King Books

SILENT KING BOOKS

SKB

Copyright © 2024 by Walter the Educator

All rights reserved. No part of this book may be reproduced in any manner whatsoever without written permission except in the case of brief quotations embodied in critical articles and reviews.

First Printing, 2024

Disclaimer
This book is a literary work; the story is not about specific persons, locations, situations, and/or circumstances unless mentioned in a historical context. Any resemblance to real persons, locations, situations, and/or circumstances is coincidental. This book is for entertainment and informational purposes only. The author and publisher offer this information without warranties expressed or implied. No matter the grounds, neither the author nor the publisher will be accountable for any losses, injuries, or other damages caused by the reader's use of this book. The use of this book acknowledges an understanding and acceptance of this disclaimer.

Celebrating the City of Makkah is a collectible souvenir book that belongs to the Celebrating Cities Book Series by Walter the Educator. Collect them all and more books at WaltertheEducator.com

MAKKAH

In the heart of the desert, where the sands whisper secrets old,

Celebrating the City of Makkah

Lies a city of splendor, its stories in golden tapestry told.

Celebrating the City of Makkah

Makkah, where the horizon embraces the sacred and the bold,

Celebrating the City of Makkah

A realm where time dances, in rhythms that endlessly unfold.

Celebrating the City of
Makkah

Oh, Makkah, cradle of the dawn, where the stars gently fall,

Celebrating the City of Makkah

Your minarets rise, eternal, answering a divine call.

Celebrating the City of Makkah

In your embrace, pilgrims gather, from valleys and from hall,

Celebrating the City of Makkah

To witness the Kaaba's grandeur, to feel the spirit's enthrall.

Celebrating the City of
Makkah

The mountains of Makkah stand like guardians, ancient and wise,

Celebrating the City of Makkah

Their peaks kiss the heavens, where celestial whispers arise.

Celebrating the City of Makkah

In their shadows, memories linger, of prophets' earnest cries,

Celebrating the City of
Makkah

Echoes of faith and devotion, that time itself defies.

Celebrating the City of
Makkah

Through bustling souks and winding streets, the essence of life flows,

Celebrating the City of Makkah

A symphony of cultures, where every heart truly knows.

Celebrating the City of
Makkah

The scent of oud and jasmine, where every fragrance grows,

Celebrating the City of Makkah

In Makkah's vibrant tapestry, every thread brightly glows.

Celebrating the City of
Makkah

Zamzam's waters, pure and clear, a gift from the divine,

Celebrating the City of
Makkah

A wellspring of sustenance, where hope and faith entwine.

Celebrating the City of
Makkah

From Hagar's steadfast footsteps, a miracle, a sign,

Celebrating the City of Makkah

In every drop, a blessing, in every sip, a shrine.

Celebrating the City of
Makkah

Beneath the Arabian sun, Makkah's beauty takes its flight,

Celebrating the City of Makkah

Golden hues of twilight, merging day into night.

Celebrating the City of
Makkah

In the sacred precincts, a luminance, a celestial light,

Celebrating the City of
Makkah

Guiding souls in reverence, in a journey of pure delight.

Celebrating the City of
Makkah

The call to prayer, a melody, that drifts upon the air,

Celebrating the City of Makkah

Uniting hearts and spirits, in a moment rich and rare.

Celebrating the City of
Makkah

From distant lands, they gather, to bow, to kneel, to share,

Celebrating the City of Makkah

In Makkah's embrace, their souls stripped of worldly care.

Celebrating the City of Makkah

Oh, Makkah, city of light, where history and future meet,

Celebrating the City of Makkah

Your streets have felt the footsteps of the faithful and the fleet.

Celebrating the City of
Makkah

In your arms, the weary find solace, and the lost find their feet,

Celebrating the City of Makkah

A sanctuary of peace, where love and devotion greet.

Celebrating the City of
Makkah

The pilgrims' chants, a harmony, that rises with the dawn,

Celebrating the City of Makkah

In circles around the Kaaba, in reverence, they are drawn.

Celebrating the City of Makkah

From every corner of the earth, in Makkah, they are reborn,

Celebrating the City of Makkah

In unity and faith, in the light of a new morn.

Celebrating the City of
Makkah

The seasons come and go, yet Makkah remains the same,

Celebrating the City of Makkah

A beacon of eternal truth, a flame that does not wane.

Celebrating the City of
Makkah

In its sacred bounds, every soul finds a name,

Celebrating the City of Makkah

In the annals of devotion, inscribed without shame.

Celebrating the City of
Makkah

Oh, Makkah, you are more than stone, more than earth or sky,

Celebrating the City of Makkah

A testament to faith, where the human spirit can fly.

Celebrating the City of
Makkah

In your sacred precincts, every tear, every sigh,

Celebrating the City of Makkah

Is a prayer, a hope, that reaches the Most High.

Celebrating the City of Makkah

ABOUT THE CREATOR

Walter the Educator is one of the pseudonyms for Walter Anderson. Formally educated in Chemistry, Business, and Education, he is an educator, an author, a diverse entrepreneur, and he is the son of a disabled war veteran. "Walter the Educator" shares his time between educating and creating. He holds interests and owns several creative projects that entertain, enlighten, enhance, and educate, hoping to inspire and motivate you.

Follow, find new works, and stay up to date
with Walter the Educator™
at WaltertheEducator.com

Milton Keynes UK
Ingram Content Group UK Ltd.
UKHW050216130724
445574UK00013B/515